THE HUMAN BODY

the world in infographics

jon richards
and ed simkins

Owl kids

CONTENTS

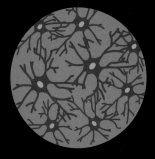
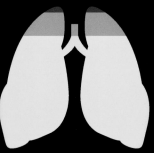

WELCOME TO THE WORLD
OF INFOGRAPHICS

Using icons, graphics, and pictograms, infographics
visualize data and information in a whole new way!

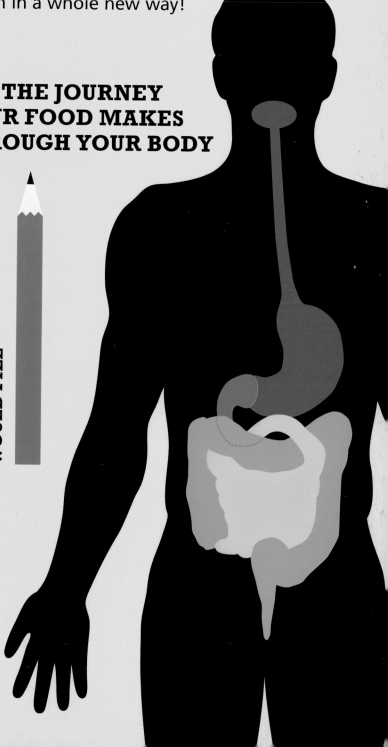

SEE THE JOURNEY YOUR FOOD MAKES THROUGH YOUR BODY

DISCOVER WHAT GOES INTO EVERY DROP OF YOUR BLOOD

FIND OUT HOW MANY PENCILS THE CARBON IN YOUR BODY WOULD FILL

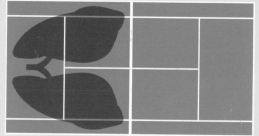

COMPARE THE SURFACE AREA OF YOUR LUNGS TO THAT OF A TENNIS COURT

BUILDING A BODY

The human body is an amazing mixture of tiny structures called cells and a whole host of chemical substances. These cells and substances combine to form a living human being.

CELL SHAPES

Cells are microscopic structures that join together to form larger parts of the human body. Each type of cell is specially shaped to perform a job. Red blood cells are doughnut-shaped and have a high surface area so they can carry a lot of oxygen. Sperm cells have long tails so they can swim. Nerve cells are long and thin and have branches that form a network and send messages.

RED BLOOD CELL

SPERM CELL

NERVE CELL

NUMBER OF CELLS IN THE BODY

100,000,000,000,000

3,000,000,000 cells die every minute (most of these are replaced).

3.2% NITROGEN

9.5% HYDROGEN

A BODY CONTAINS...

ENOUGH PHOSPHORUS TO MAKE

220

MATCHES.

ENOUGH FAT TO FORM

75

CANDLES.

18.5% CARBON

ENOUGH CARBON TO FILL ## 900 PENCILS.

ENOUGH IRON TO MAKE A NAIL THAT'S 3 IN. (7 CM) LONG.

65% OXYGEN

HOW THE BODY IS STRUCTURED

Similar types of cells join together to form structures called tissues. Different tissues join together to create organs, which link to create whole body systems.

NERVE CELL

BRAIN

NERVOUS SYSTEM

LESS THAN 4% CALCIUM, PHOSPHORUS, POTASSIUM, SULFUR, SODIUM, AND MORE

NERVE TISSUE

BONE STRUCTURE

The human body keeps its shape thanks to the skeleton, a system of bones that are connected by joints.

SKELETON

The skeleton features a central part called the axial skeleton, made up of the skull, spine, and ribs. Off these hang the bones of the limbs, which make up the appendicular skeleton.

A NEWBORN BABY HAS

270

BONES. MANY OF THESE FUSE TOGETHER AND BY ADULTHOOD THERE ARE

206

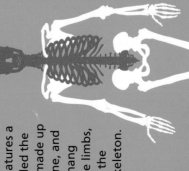

80 AXIAL BONE

126 APPENDICULAR

BONES MAKE UP ABOUT **20%** OF BODY WEIGHT.

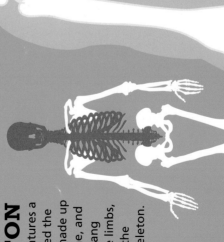

HEALING BONES

Bone tissue has the amazing ability to repair itself when damaged. The process can take as little as a few weeks.

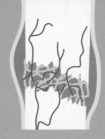
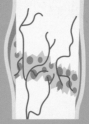

1. Just after the bone breaks, a swelling filled with clotted blood forms around it.

2. Inside the swelling, blood vessels and thin rods of bone start to grow across the break.

3. More bony tissue grows across the break, forming a hard swollen area called a callus.

4. Bone tissue grows over the callus to heal the break.

FEMUR

FEMUR

SMALLEST BONES

Found inside the ears, tiny bones called ossicles vibrate and carry sounds to the inner ear. Each bone is about 0.2–0.3 in. (5–7.75 mm) long.

ACTUAL SIZE

STAPES

INCUS

MALLEUS

LONGEST BONE

The longest bone in the body is the upper leg bone, or femur. It runs from the hip down to the top of the knee.

20 in. (50 cm)

640 MUSCLES

SKELETAL MUSCLES MAKE UP ABOUT **40%** **OF YOUR BODY WEIGHT.**

All the movements that happen in your body, from lifting a leg to smiling, are all due to a type of tissue that can contract, called muscle.

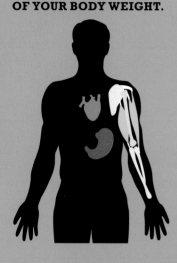

MUSCLE TYPES

There are three types of muscle in the body: skeletal, smooth, and cardiac. Skeletal muscles move the skeleton; smooth muscles perform a range of tasks, including pushing food through the gut; and the cardiac muscle powers the heart.

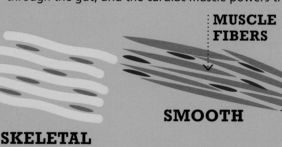

MUSCLE FIBERS

SKELETAL

SMOOTH

CARDIAC

HOW MUSCLES CONTRACT

Muscles are made up of two types of tiny filaments: thick and thin. These muscle filaments slide over each other to contract the muscle, or make the muscle shorter.

RELAXED MUSCLE

CONTRACTING MUSCLE

FULLY CONTRACTED MUSCLE

THIN FILAMENTS

THICK FILAMENTS

BONE

MUSCLE

JOINT

TENDON

BONE

TENDONS

Skeletal muscles are attached to the bones by thick cords called tendons. The joints themselves are held together by cords known as ligaments.

WORKING IN PAIRS

Muscles exert a pulling force when they contract, but they exert no force when they are relaxed, meaning they can't push. So, in order to move a body part back and forth, muscles need to work in pairs. One muscle contracts, or pulls, while another relaxes. Muscles that work together like this are called antagonistic pairs.

TENDON

BICEPS
CONTRACTED

BICEPS
RELAXED

TRICEPS
CONTRACTED

TRICEPS
RELAXED

TENDON

GLUTEUS MAXIMUS

The name of the largest muscle in the body, found in each buttock.

The **27** bones in your **hand** are controlled by tendons and more than **30** muscles located in the **hand** and **forearm**.

HOW MUCH CAN A MUSCLE MOVE ?

A muscle can contract to **85%** of its relaxed length.

100% relaxed

It can stretch to **120%** of its relaxed length.

ON THE
SURFACE

The outside of your body is covered with skin, hair, and nails. Skin forms a protective layer, while hair keeps some body parts warm and nails help you grip objects.

SWEAT GLANDS

Your skin is covered with up to

4 MILLION

sweat glands. The greatest concentrations are found on the palms and the soles, where there are up to

2260 per square inch (350 per square centimeter).

0.4 in.

(1 cm)

SKIN

The largest organ in the human body is the skin. New skin cells form at the bottom of the skin's outer layer. They then move to the surface, die, and harden, before flaking off and being replaced.

THERE'S ENOUGH SKIN ON AN ADULT HUMAN TO COVER ABOUT **21.5 ft.² (2 m²).**

SKIN MAKES UP ABOUT 12% OF YOUR BODY WEIGHT.

THAT'S NEARLY

20 lb. (9 kg)

IN A 165 LB. (75 KG) ADULT.

YOU LOSE ABOUT
50,000

flakes of dead skin every minute. That's

40 lb. (18 kg)

in a lifetime

HAIR CAN GROW ABOUT **0.6 in. (15 mm)** A MONTH. THAT'S **7.2 in. (180 mm)** IN A YEAR.

0.6 in. (15 mm)

100,000

THE AVERAGE NUMBER OF HAIRS ON THE HUMAN HEAD

HAIR

The style of a person's hair is determined by the shape of the hair's cross-section.

STRAIGHT

WAVY

CURLY

AN ADULT WILL SWEAT ABOUT 2 CUPS (0.5 LITERS) PER DAY.

CHRISTINE WALTON FROM THE UNITED STATES HAS FINGERNAILS THAT MEASURE

19.75 ft. (602 cm)

IN TOTAL—THREE TIMES LONGER THAN A VERY TALL PERSON!

NAILS

The hard substance that makes up nails is called keratin. It is also found in skin cells and in hair.

BREATHE IN,
BREATHE OUT

Oxygen in the air is vital for life. Two sacs inside your chest, called lungs, take oxygen out of the air every time you breathe in.

BREATHING RATES

EXERCISING
80
BREATHS PER MINUTE

RESTING
15
BREATHS PER MINUTE

2,906 gallons
The number of gallons (11,000 liters) a person will breathe on average each day.

LUNGS HAVE ABOUT
1,491 mi. (2,400 km)
OF AIRWAYS INSIDE THEM. THAT'S THE DISTANCE FROM LONDON TO ATHENS.

INHALE
The diaphragm contracts and flattens, and the muscles between the ribs contract, pulling the rib cage up and out. This draws air into the lungs, through tubes called airways.

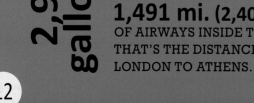

THE SURFACE AREA INSIDE THE LUNGS IS

754 ft.²
(70 m²)

THAT'S THE SAME AS HALF A TENNIS COURT.

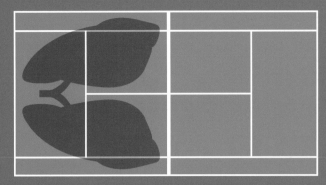

THIS LARGE AREA IS CREATED BY UP TO

500,000,000

TINY SAC STRUCTURES, CALLED ALVEOLI.

EXHALE

Air flows through the airways until it reaches the alveoli, which are surrounded by tiny blood vessels. The diaphragm and the muscles between the ribs then relax, squeezing air out of the lungs.

ALVEOLI

When air reaches the alveoli, oxygen travels into the blood vessels, while carbon dioxide passes the other way.

WHAT'S IN THE AIR WE BREATHE?

INHALED

79% NITROGEN
20% OXYGEN
0.04% CARBON DIOXIDE
TINY AMOUNTS OF
WATER VAPOR AND
VARIOUS GASES

EXHALED

79% NITROGEN
16% OXYGEN
4% CARBON DIOXIDE,
WATER VAPOR, AND
OTHER GASES

13

EATING

Running from the mouth to the anus is a long passageway. Its role is to break down the food you eat and take out all the nutrients your body needs to operate, grow, and repair itself.

FOOD IS CHEWED INSIDE THE MOUTH.

MOUTH

6–10 SECONDS

ESOPHAGUS

1–4

THE STOMACH CHURNS AND BREAKS DOWN FOOD TO MUSH.

YOUR MOUTH WILL PRODUCE NEARLY

10,567 gallons (40,000 liters)

OF SALIVA IN A LIFETIME.

THAT'S ABOUT 4–6 CUPS (1–1.5 LITERS) EVERY DAY.

30 ft. (9 m)

THE LENGTH OF THE ENTIRE DIGESTIVE SYSTEM FROM MOUTH TO ANUS IF STRETCHED OUT STRAIGHT

STOMACH

LARGE INTESTINE

SMALL INTESTINE

ANUS

4 HOURS

2 HOURS

14 HOURS

YOUR INTESTINES PRODUCE ABOUT 8.5 CUPS (2 LITERS) OF GAS EVERY DAY.

THE SMALL INTESTINE ABSORBS MOST OF THE NUTRIENTS.

An adult will produce up to 0.6 LB. (0.25 KG) of solid waste a day.

WHAT'S SOLID WASTE MADE OF?

75% WATER
25% SOLID MATTER

Of the solid matter, 30% is dead bacteria, 30% indigestible material (such as cellulose), 10–20% cholesterol and other fats, 10–20% inorganic substances (such as calcium phosphate), and 10–20% proteins.

TEETH

Teeth are covered in a tough substance called enamel, which is the hardest material in the body. Each tooth is shaped to perform a specific job.

MOLAR
GRINDING AND CHEWING

PREMOLAR
GRINDING AND CHEWING

CANINE
PIERCING AND HOLDING

INCISOR
SLICING AND TEARING

PERISTALSIS

Food is pushed through the gut by waves of muscle contractions, called peristalsis.

BLOOD AND
THE HEART

THE HEART PUMPS ABOUT **3,600 GALLONS (13,640 LITERS)** OF BLOOD AROUND THE BODY EVERY DAY.

Blood carries oxygen from the lungs and nutrients from the gut to every cell in the body. These are used to produce energy and repair damaged cells.

HOW MUCH BLOOD?

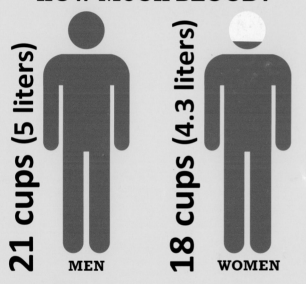

21 cups (5 liters)
MEN

18 cups (4.3 liters)
WOMEN

WHAT'S IN BLOOD?

Blood is made up of three types of blood cells: red, white, and platelets. They all float about in a straw-colored liquid called plasma.

YOUR BLOOD CONTAINS UP TO **30,000,000,000** RED BLOOD CELLS.

UP TO **2,000,000** ARE MADE EVERY SECOND.

54.3%
PLASMA

0.7%
WHITE CELLS AND PLATELETS

45%
RED BLOOD CELLS

THE HEART

At the center of the blood system is the heart. It squeezes rhythmically to push blood through a network of tubes, called blood vessels. Each heartbeat has four phases.

THE HEART WILL AVERAGE **70 BEATS PER MINUTE**—ABOUT **100,000 BEATS PER DAY.**

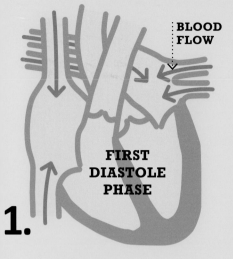

BLOOD FLOW

1. FIRST DIASTOLE PHASE

2. FIRST SYSTOLE PHASE

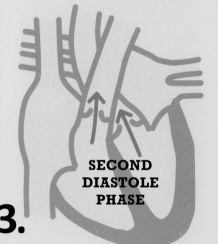

3. SECOND DIASTOLE PHASE

4. SECOND SYSTOLE PHASE

AN ADULT HAS UP TO **62,137 mi. (100,000 km)** OF BLOOD VESSELS—ENOUGH TO STRETCH AROUND THE WORLD 2.5 TIMES.

DEFENDING THE BODY

White blood cells help to defend the body from infection and disease. Some of them "eat up" foreign invaders in a process called phagocytosis.

1. THE CELL SENSES BACTERIA NEARBY AND MOVES TOWARD THEM.

2. THE CELL WRAPS ITS MEMBRANE AROUND THE BACTERIA.

3. THE CELL DIGESTS, OR BREAKS DOWN, THE BACTERIA.

THE SENSES

Sense organs all over your body detect changes in the world around you and send signals to the brain. The organs detect pressure, heat, colors, lights, sounds, tastes, and smells.

RANGE OF AUDIBLE SOUND FREQUENCIES IN HERTZ (HZ)

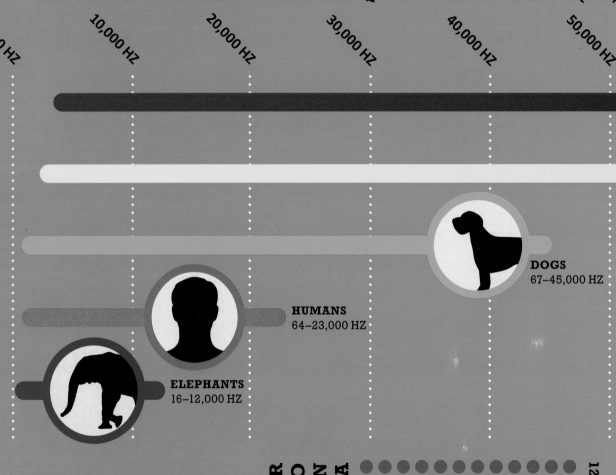

0 HZ   10,000 HZ   20,000 HZ   30,000 HZ   40,000 HZ   50,000 HZ

DOGS
67–45,000 HZ

HUMANS
64–23,000 HZ

ELEPHANTS
16–12,000 HZ

THE RETINA

The back of the eye is called the retina. It is covered with millions of special cells, called rods and cones. Rods detect black and white in low light, while cones can detect all colors in bright light.

NUMBER OF RODS TO CONES IN THE RETINA

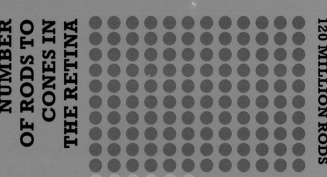

120 MILLION RODS

6 MILLION CONES

Your **nose** contains **10–20 million** smell receptor cells and these can detect more than **3,500** different odors.

70,000 HZ

80,000 HZ

90,000 HZ

100,000 HZ

110,000 HZ

HZ

BATS
2,000–110,000 HZ

MICE
1,000–91,000 HZ

HOW SENSITIVE?

Your skin is packed with touch receptors. These receptors send signals along the nervous system to a part of the brain called the sensory area. Some body parts have more touch receptors than others. This figure shows what you would look like if your body was shaped according to how sensitive each body part is, with the more sensitive parts being the largest.

YOUR **TONGUE**, **LIPS**, AND **FINGERS** WOULD BE YOUR **LARGEST** PARTS, WHILE YOUR **NECK** AND **BACK** WOULD BE **VERY SMALL.**

NERVOUS
SYSTEM

Running through your body is a network of nerve fibers. At the center of this network is the brain, which receives information from your senses and tells the body how to react.

THE BRAIN CONTAINS
1,000,000,000,000
NERVE CELLS.

IRONED OUT FLAT, THE OUTER LAYER OF THE BRAIN WOULD COVER **324 IN.^{2} (2,090 CM^2)—** ABOUT THE AREA OF THREE TENNIS RACKET HEADS.

PRIMARY MOTOR AREA CONTROLS VOLUNTARY MOVEMENTS

ANTERIOR SPEECH AREA INVOLVED IN PRODUCING SPEECH

SECONDARY MOTOR AREA AND SENSORY AREA HELPS TO COORDINATE MOVEMENTS

BRAIN GROWTH

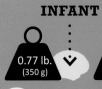

INFANT

0.77 lb. (350 g)

1 YEAR

2.2 lb. (1 kg)

PUBERTY

2.9 lb. (1.3 kg)

ADULT

3.3 lb. (1.5 kg)

PRIMARY SENSORY AREA
PROCESSES INFORMATION
ABOUT TOUCH

THE SPEED OF
A NERVE SIGNAL

A nerve signal travels as fast as
a bullet train. It takes about
0.02 seconds for a signal to travel
from your foot to your brain.

POSTERIOR SPEECH AREA
ALLOWS US TO UNDERSTAND
SPEECH AND WRITING

SECONDARY VISUAL AREA
DETECTS COMPLEX
VISUAL IMAGES

PRIMARY VISUAL AREA
DETECTS SIMPLE
VISUAL IMAGES

**SECONDARY
AUDITORY AREA**
RECOGNIZES MUSIC

PRIMARY AUDITORY AREA
PROCESSES SOUNDS
FROM OUR EARS

MOTOR
AREA

Each body part is
controlled by a section
of the primary motor
area—the larger the
section, the more control
the brain has over that
body part. The figure on the
right shows what a person would
look like if their body parts were
proportional in size to their section
of the primary motor area.

2%

**THE BRAIN MAKES UP
JUST 2 PERCENT OF THE
WEIGHT OF A HUMAN BODY.**

THE HUMAN HOME

You are not alone! The human body is home to billions of other living organisms, from tiny bacteria to long tapeworms. Some are harmful, but many are essential to your health.

BACTERIA FOUND INSIDE THE GUT OUTNUMBER HUMAN BODY CELLS

10 TO 1.

HEAD LICE

Head lice are about 0.1 in. (3 mm) long and feed by biting the scalp and sucking blood through the wound.

 ⟵······ **ACTUAL SIZE**

MALARIA

One of the deadliest diseases, malaria, is caused by Plasmodium parasites in the blood. These parasites are carried by mosquitoes.

600 different species of bacteria live inside a human mouth.

These trillions of bacteria help to break down the chemicals in your food into simpler substances that your body can absorb.

MORE THAN

750,000

PEOPLE DIE FROM MALARIA EVERY YEAR AROUND THE WORLD

YOUR SKIN IS HOME TO ABOUT **1,000** DIFFERENT SPECIES OF BACTERIA.

The beef tapeworm can grow up to

39 ft. (12 m)

long inside the human intestine, the equivalent to the height of seven average-sized adult humans.

It is thought that there are **500–1,000** different **species** of **bacteria** living in the human **intestine**.

TAPEWORM EGGS HAVE BEEN FOUND IN EGYPTIAN MUMMIES, DATING FROM **2000 BCE**.

REPRODUCTION

To create a new human being, two tiny cells—a sperm cell (spermatozoon) from the father and an egg cell (ovum) from the mother—have to meet and fuse together. To do this, the sperm cells need to travel through the uterus and into the correct Fallopian tube.

300,000,000,000 ARE RELEASED ON AVERAGE AT EJACULATION.

NUMBER OF SPERM AT VARIOUS STAGES OF THE JOURNEY TO FERTILIZATION

10,000 ENTER THE UTERUS.

3,000 REACH THE TOP OF THE UTERUS.

1,500 ENTER THE CORRECT FALLOPIAN TUBE.

300 REACH THE EGG CELL.

1 FERTILIZES THE EGG CELL.

RELEASING EGGS

A woman is born with a huge number of egg cells, but only a small number of these will develop. Just one is released each month to be fertilized by sperm from a man.

500 START TO DEVELOP AT PUBERTY.

1 IS RELEASED EVERY 28 DAYS.

750,000 EGG CELLS ARE PRESENT AT BIRTH.

FUSING

Once a sperm reaches the egg cell, it burrows through the egg's outer layers and fuses with the egg.

SPERM

EGG

CELL NUCLEUS

SPERM BURROWS THROUGH OUTER LAYERS.

0.002 in.
(55 micrometers)

The length of a human sperm. An egg cell is 0.005 in. (120 micrometers) across.

GROWING

Soon after fertilization, the cell starts to multiply and form a body. After some time, the cells begin to specialize, creating different body parts, such as fingers and eyes.

35 DAYS

45 DAYS

49 DAYS

56 DAYS

70 DAYS

105 DAYS

GROWING UP

A human will grow until he or she reaches a physical peak, when the body is performing at its best. This is usually at about the age of 25. After that, the body's ability to perform certain tasks starts to decline.

BODY PROPORTION CHANGES

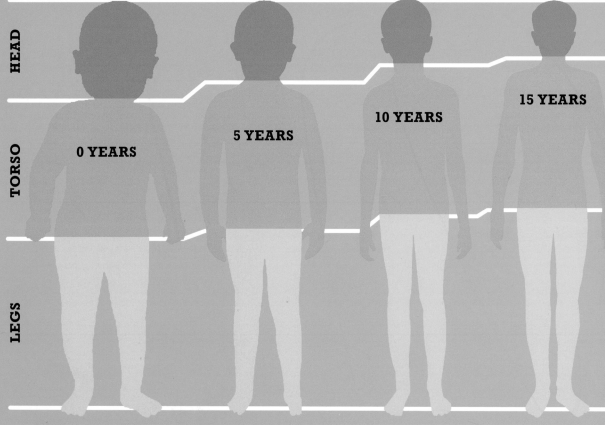

HEAD

TORSO

LEGS

0 YEARS

5 YEARS

10 YEARS

15 YEARS

GROWING BODY

People don't grow at the same rate. There are spurts of growth during puberty. These occur at the ages of about 12 for girls and 14 for boys.

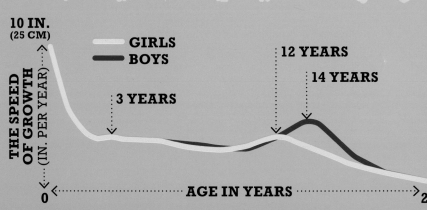

10 IN.
(25 CM)

THE SPEED OF GROWTH (IN. PER YEAR)

GIRLS
BOYS

3 YEARS

12 YEARS

14 YEARS

0

AGE IN YEARS

20

THE EFFECTS OF AGE...

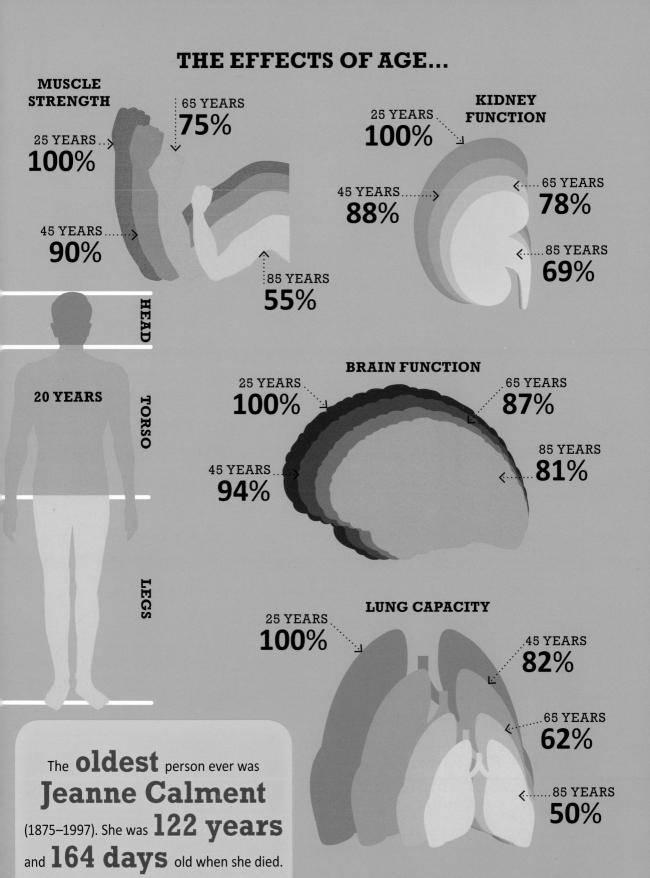

MUSCLE STRENGTH

25 YEARS... **100%**

65 YEARS **75%**

45 YEARS..... **90%**

85 YEARS **55%**

KIDNEY FUNCTION

25 YEARS... **100%**

45 YEARS........ **88%**

65 YEARS **78%**

85 YEARS **69%**

HEAD

20 YEARS

TORSO

LEGS

BRAIN FUNCTION

25 YEARS **100%**

65 YEARS **87%**

45 YEARS **94%**

85 YEARS **81%**

LUNG CAPACITY

25 YEARS **100%**

45 YEARS **82%**

65 YEARS **62%**

85 YEARS **50%**

The **oldest** person ever was **Jeanne Calment** (1875–1997). She was **122 years** and **164 days** old when she died.

SPARE PARTS

Body parts wear out or break through injury, disease, or old age. Many can be repaired, or, if the damage is serious enough, replaced with natural or artificial parts.

CORNEA

The cornea at the front of the eye can be replaced entirely or in part with a transplant from a dead person.

COCHLEAR IMPLANT

Also called a bionic ear, this device has microphones to collect sounds and convert them into electrical signals to send to the brain.

LUNGS

A pair of diseased lungs can be replaced with a pair donated by a dead person.

HEART

A human heart can be transplanted from a dead person or even from a pig!

PANCREAS

A pancreatic transplant may be carried out on a person suffering from diabetes with a whole organ from a dead person or part of the organ from a living donor.

KIDNEY

This is the most common form of transplant, where one or both of the kidneys are replaced with those from a living or dead donor.

LIVER

The liver can be replaced with a whole transplant from a dead person or part of the organ from a living donor.

INTESTINE

Parts of the small or large intestine can be replaced if they have been damaged by disease.

ARTIFICIAL HIP

Metal and ceramic hip pieces replace the worn parts from the leg and hip joint.

PROSTHETIC LIMB

If an arm or leg has to be removed, or amputated, then the whole limb can be replaced with a prosthetic limb. Scientists have even developed prosthetic arms and legs that can be controlled by a person's thoughts.

1967

The year of the first heart transplant. It was performed by Christiaan Barnard at a hospital in Cape Town, South Africa.

2011

The year of the first double leg transplant, performed by a team of surgeons at a hospital in Valencia, Spain.

BLOOD VESSELS

Blood vessels can be replaced with transplants from a living person, or they can be moved and grafted to replace damaged vessels elsewhere in the body.

SKIN

Skin can be taken from one part of the body and grafted to another to cover a serious wound.

TENDONS AND LIGAMENTS

These cord-like structures can be replaced with parts from elsewhere in the body or donations from dead or living donors.

BONE MARROW

This is found inside many bones and plays an important role in creating red blood cells. It can be replaced with a donation from a living donor.

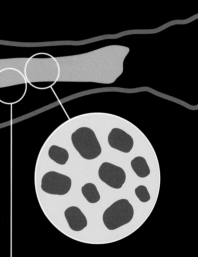

GLOSSARY

Amputate
To remove a body part that is diseased or badly damaged.

Appendicular skeleton
The part of the skeleton formed by the shoulders, arms, hips, and legs.

Audible
A sound that can be detected by the ear. Different ranges of sound are audible to different animals.

Axial skeleton
The central part of the skeleton, formed by the skull, backbone, and ribs.

Blood vessels
Tubes that carry blood around the body. There are three kinds of blood vessels: arteries, which carry blood from the heart; capillaries, which carry blood from the arteries to individual cells in the body; and veins, which carry blood from the capillaries back to the heart.

Cell
The smallest building block of life. All animals and plants are made out of cells. The human body contains about 10 trillion cells.

Organ
A group of body tissues that work together to carry out particular jobs in the body. The heart, brain, stomach, and skin are all examples of organs in the human body.

Contract
To shorten in length. Muscles contract in order to exert a pulling force.

Diaphragm
A sheet of muscle that sits across the bottom of the ribs and helps you breathe.

Graft
To move tissue from one part of the body to another. When a person has badly damaged skin, doctors may graft skin from another part of the body to mend the damaged area.

Keratin
A tough substance that is an important part of the skin, nails, and hair. It is also found in the scales of reptiles and shells of tortoises and turtles.

Ligaments
Strong, cord-like tissues that connect one bone to another.

Muscle filament
Thin strands of muscle tissue that slide over each other when the muscle contracts.

Organism
A living thing. An organism may be large, such as a human, or tiny, such as a bacterium.

Plasma
A straw-colored liquid that makes up more than 50 percent of blood. Red and white blood cells are carried in the plasma.

Puberty
A period of body development that starts at around age 12 in girls and 14 in boys. During puberty, the body grows very quickly and changes shape, and the sexual organs develop.

Relaxed

A state in which muscles are not exerting a pulling force. Relaxed muscles are longer than muscles that are contracting.

Retina

An area at the back of the eye that contains special cells that detect light. The retina sends information to the brain along the optic nerve.

Saliva

A watery substance produced inside the mouth. Saliva contains chemicals that start the process of digestion as we chew our food.

Species

A group of organisms that are very similar and can reproduce with each other to produce fertile offspring. All living beings belong to one particular species.

System

A group of organs in the body that work together to carry out particular jobs. One organ may work for several different body systems. For instance, the liver works for the digestive system and the circulatory system.

Phagocytosis

The process by which a cell traps and then destroys bacteria in the body. Some white blood cells kill harmful bacteria through phagocytosis.

Tendons

Strong, cord-like tissues that connect muscles to bones.

Tissue

A group of similar cells in the body that does one particular job.

Torso

The part of the body to which the limbs and neck are attached. The torso contains most of the body's important organs.

Resources

MORE GRAPHICS:
www.visualinformation.info
A website that contains a whole host of infographic material on subjects as diverse as natural history, science, sport, and computer games.

www.coolinfographics.com
A collection of infographics and data visualizations from other online resources, magazines, and newspapers.

www.dailyinfographic.com
A comprehensive collection of infographics on an enormous range of topics that is updated every single day!

MORE INFO:
www.kidshealth.org
Answers to all the questions you might have about how your body changes as you grow up.

http://faculty.washington.edu/chudler/neurok.html
A website packed with fascinating information about the brain for kids and adults.

The following sources were consulted to create this book:
Encyclopedia Britannica; *Human Anatomy and Physiology*, 3rd Edition; Louisiana State University; *Science Daily*; World Health Organization

INDEX

 OWL kids Publisher of Chirp, chickaDEE and OWL
www.owlkidsbooks.com

Published in North America in 2013
© 2012 Wayland

Owlkids Books acknowledges the financial support of the Canada Council for the Arts, the Ontario Arts Council, the Government of Canada through the Canada Book Fund (CBF) and the Government of Ontario through the Ontario Media Development Corporation's Book Initiative for our publishing activities.

Published in Canada by
Owlkids Books Inc.
10 Lower Spadina Avenue
Toronto, ON M5V 2Z2

Published in the United States by
Owlkids Books Inc.
1700 Fourth Street
Berkeley, CA 94710

Library and Archives Canada Cataloguing in Publication

Richards, Jon, 1970-
 The human body / written by Jon Richards ; illustrated by Ed Simkins.

(The world in infographics)
Includes bibliographical references and index.
ISBN 978-1-926973-93-7

 1. Human body--Juvenile literature. I. Simkins, Ed II. Title. III. Series: World in infographics

QP37.R54 2013 j612 C2012-908497-2

Library of Congress Control Number: 2013930495

Manufactured in Hong Kong, in February 2013, by Printing Express Ltd.
Job #13-01-018

A B C D E F